EXPLORING THE DIVINE

THE 33 KOTI DEVATAS AND BEYOND

DR. JAGADEESH PILLAI

|| Dedicated to all Wisdom Seekers Around The World"

Contents

Contents

Prayer

"Om Asato Maa Sadgamaya,Tamaso Maa Jyotir Gamaya,Mrityor Maa Amritam Gamaya, Om Shantih, Shantih, Shantih"

The true meaning of this mantra is: OM guide me from the unreal to the real, from darkness to light, and from mortality to immortality.
OM Peace, Peace, Peace.

About The Author

Dr. Jagadeesh Pillai is a renowned Guinness World Record holder, writer, and researcher hailing from Varanasi, also known as the abode of Lord Shiva. With a Ph.D. in Vedic Science and a range of creative ideas and achievements, he is a true polymath. He is the author of more than 100 books including Research Publications. Although his roots can be traced back to Kerala, the people of Varanasi hold him in high regard and affectionately consider him one of their own.

Dr. Pillai has achieved four Guinness World Records in the following subjects:

1. "Script to Screen" - In this record, Dr. Pillai produced and directed an animation film within the shortest time possible, breaking the previous record set by Canadians. He has also received numerous national and international awards and recognitions for this achievement.

2. Longest Line of Postcards - For this record, Dr. Pillai created a line of 16,300 postcards on the occasion of the 163rd anniversary of Indian Postal Day. The event also included a questionnaire about the Indian flag.

3. Largest Poster Awareness Campaign - Dr. Pillai designed an awareness campaign on the subject of "Beti Bachao - Beti Padhao" (Save the Girl Child - Educate the Girl Child) to achieve this record.

4. Largest Envelope - In tribute to the Indian Prime Minister's "Make in India" initiative, Dr. Pillai created a 4000 square meter envelope using waste paper to achieve this record.

5. Attempted - 70000 Candles on a 210 kg Cake - To celebrate the 70th Indian Independence Day, Dr. Pillai attempted to light 70,000 candles on a 210 kg cake, which was recorded in World Records India.

6. Attempted - Documentary on Dhamek Stupa of Sarnath in 17 Languages - Dr. Pillai attempted to create a documentary on the Dhamek Stupa of Sarnath, dubbing it in 17 different languages. The result of this attempt is currently awaiting confirmation from the Guinness World Records.

Dr. Pillai is skilled in teaching the Bhagavad Gita, a Hindu scripture, and is popular among young people. He has helped many young people improve their lives through his motivational teachings.

In addition to teaching, he has composed and sung numerous Sanskrit Bhajans and patriotic songs.

He has also written and directed several short films and documentaries for awareness campaigns, and has volunteered with the police in both UP and Kerala to spread awareness about various issues through videos and photography.

He has a goal of writing thousands of books on Indian culture, Indian temples, and the lives of extraordinary people. Incredibly, he has produced and directed over 100 documentaries about the city of Varanasi, all on his own.

He has also helped and guided more than 25 boys and girls to achieve world records through creative and innovative methods. He is a multifaceted person who uses his intellect and the blessings given to him by God to excel in various areas. He is both a teacher and a student, always learning and teaching, and is able to master any subject he comes across.

He is a selfless social activist and motivational speaker who has overcome struggles and failures to become a successful and enthusiastic individual with a rich life experience.

In addition to his work with the Bhagavad Gita, he is also an efficient Tarot card reader, Astro-Vastu consultant, and a talented singer and composer. He has sung the entire Ram Charita Manas and Bhagavad Gita in his own compositions, and has sung the phrase "Lokah Samastha Sukhino Bhavantu" in 50 different languages. He is currently working on a detailed and scientific study of Vedas, Upanishads, Puranas, and the Bhagavad Gita. He has also composed and sung the Hanuman Chalisa and Gayatri Mantra in 108 and 1008 different compositions, respectively.

<u>Awards</u>

Four Times Guinness World Records, Winner of Mahatma Gandhi Vishwa Shanti Puraskar , Mahatma Gandhi Global Peace Ambassador, Kashi Ratna Award, Dr. APJ Abdul Kalam Motivational Person of the Year 2017, Mother Teresa Award, Indira Gandhi Priyadarshini Award, Bharat Vikas Ratna Award, Udyog Ratna Award, Vigyan Prasar Award, Poorvanchal Ratn Samman.

Preface

The concept of 33 koti devatas has been around for millennia, and its origin and meaning remain a great mystery even today. Legends of 33 koti devatas fill Hindu mythology, and their presence and influence are intertwined with that of both traditional hindu scripture and natural forces. This book sets out to explore and explain these 33 koti devatas, uncovering their connections between the physical elements, spirituality and ancient prophecies.

Throughout these 21 chapters, I have endeavored to outline a thorough and comprehensive exploration of 33 koti devatas and their significance. From the earliest indications of their existence to the visible and invisible relationships that they form with their environment, this book is designed to provide an engaging and in-depth examination into the fascinating world of 33 koti devatas.

To begin this exploration, chapter one will provide a brief introduction to 33 koti devatas, outlining their history and place in hindu mythology. Subsequent chapters will delve deeper into details, including the unique characteristics and personalities of each of the 33 koti devatas as well as how they interact with people, places and spiritual forces. Additionally, I provide insight into significant moments in their existence and how their mythology fits into traditional hindu culture.

Through this book, it is my intent to connect knowledge and understanding of 33 koti devatas and also other deity concepts to everyday life and to offer inspiration and guidance on how to incorporate their meaning into every day practice. It is my sincere hope that this book will be a source of discovery and enlightenment, reminding us of the power of the invisible forces that surround us.

CHAPTER ONE

Introduction to the 33 Koti devatas

The term "33 crore devatas" (33 crore is a large number equal to 330 million) is sometimes used to refer to all of the gods and goddesses in the Hindu pantheon. It can also be used to refer more specifically to the 33 principal deities who are believed to preside over the 33 divisions of the earthly plane. These deities are associated with various aspects of life and nature, and are believed to have the power to influence the world and bring blessings to those who honour them. It is common for Hindus to pray to or seek the blessings of these deities in order to achieve specific goals or to overcome problems in their lives.

In Hinduism, the concept of 33 koti devatas refers to the 33 types of deities that are mentioned in the Vedas and other Hindu scriptures. These deities are believed to preside over different aspects of life and the natural world, and are often invoked by Hindus in prayer and ritual to seek blessings and assistance.

According to the Vedas, the 33 koti devatas are divided into three main categories: the Vasus, the Rudras, and the

Adityas. The Vasus are eight deities who represent elements of the natural world, such as earth, water, fire, air, and ether. The Rudras are 11 deities who are associated with the vital energies or "pranas" that animate the human body, as well as the human soul. The Adityas are 12 deities who represent the months of the year and are responsible for the passage of time.

In addition to these three groups, the Vedas also mention two other deities: Indra, who is associated with electricity and is considered the king of the gods, and Prajapati, who is also known as the "Yajna" and is believed to benefit mankind through the purification of the air, water, rain, and vegetables.

According to Hindu belief, the master of these 33 koti devatas is the supreme deity, Mahadeva or Ishwar, who is to be worshipped above all others. In the 14th Kanda of the Shatpath Brahman, it is said that the Mahadeva is the ultimate source of all power and knowledge, and that he alone should be worshipped and revered. In this way, the concept of the 33 koti devatas is an important part of Hinduism and is deeply intertwined with the belief in a single, all-powerful deity who governs the world and all that is within it.

In Hinduism, the concept of the 33 koti devatas is an important part of the belief system and is often referred to in prayer, ritual, and worship. These deities are seen as powerful forces that can bring blessings and assistance to those who honor them, and are believed to have a significant influence on the natural world and on the lives of humans.

Hindus often pray to or make offerings to the 33 koti devatas in order to seek their help and guidance in various aspects of life. For example, a person might pray to the Vasus for assistance with a problem related to the natural world, such as a drought or a natural disaster. Similarly, a person might seek the blessings of the Rudras for help with health issues or for protection against harm. And the Adityas might be invoked for help with matters related to time, such as achieving success or overcoming challenges.

In addition to being invoked in prayer and ritual, the 33 koti devatas are also an important part of Hindu mythology and storytelling. Many of the deities are featured in myths and legends that are passed down from generation to generation, and they are often depicted in art and literature as powerful and awe-inspiring beings.

The concept of the 33 koti devatas plays a central role in Hinduism and is an integral part of the religion's belief system and cultural traditions.

CHAPTER TWO

The Vasus: the eight deities of natural elements

The Vasus are a group of eight deities in Hinduism who are associated with elements of the natural world. They are called Vasus because they are believed to be the abode of all that lives, moves, or exists.

The Vasus are a group of eight deities in Hinduism who are associated with elements of the natural world. They are called Vasus because they are believed to be the abode of all that lives, moves, or exists. These deities are revered for their role in sustaining and nourishing the world, and are seen as protectors and guardians of the natural order.

The first Vasu is known as Apa, who is associated with the element of water. He is revered as the god of rivers and streams, and is often depicted as a gentle and nurturing deity who helps to provide for the basic needs of the people.

The second Vasu is known as Dhruva, who is associated with the element of the earth. He is revered as the god of stability and support, and is often depicted as a strong and reliable deity who helps to provide a foundation for the world.

The third Vasu is known as Soma, who is associated with the element of the moon. He is revered as the god of fertility and rejuvenation, and is often depicted as a gentle and soothing deity who helps to bring balance and harmony to the world.

The fourth Vasu is known as Anila, who is associated with the element of air. He is revered as the god of wind and movement, and is often depicted as a powerful and swift deity who helps to bring freshness and vitality to the world.

The fifth Vasu is known as Anala, who is associated with the element of fire. He is revered as the god of heat and energy, and is often depicted as a fierce and radiant deity who helps to bring warmth and light to the world.

The sixth Vasu is known as Pratyusha, who is associated with the element of the dawn. He is revered as the god of new beginnings and renewal, and is often depicted as a hopeful and optimistic deity who helps to bring new opportunities and possibilities to the world.

The seventh Vasu is known as Prabhasa, who is associated with the element of the sun. He is revered as the god of light and illumination, and is often depicted as a radiant and shining deity who helps to bring warmth and vitality to the world.

The eighth and final Vasu is known as Dhara, who is associated with the element of the earth. He is revered as the god of support and sustenance, and is often depicted as a strong and reliable deity who helps to provide for the basic needs of the people.

In Hindu mythology, the Vasus are revered as powerful and benevolent deities who are responsible for maintaining balance and harmony in the world. They are seen as protectors and guardians, who help to guide and support the people on their journey through life. Whether it is through providing nourishment and sustenance, or through bringing new beginnings and renewal, the Vasus are revered as powerful and benevolent deities who help to enrich and enrich the lives of those who honor and worship them.

CHAPTER THREE

The Adityas: The Twelve Deities of the Sun

The Adityas are a group of twelve solar deities in Hindu mythology, and are considered to be the sons of Aditi, the personification of infinite space and the mother of all gods. These deities are associated with the sun, and are revered for their ability to bring light, warmth, and life to the world.

The first Aditya is known as Aryaman, who is associated with the concept of social order and the maintenance of dharma. He is often depicted as a noble and just ruler, who ensures that the laws of society are followed and upheld.

The second Aditya is known as Bhaga, who is associated with the concept of wealth and prosperity. He is revered as the god of abundance and good fortune, and is often depicted as a generous and kind-hearted deity who helps to provide for the needs of the people.

The third Aditya is known as Daksha, who is associated

with the concept of power and strength. He is revered as the god of leadership and authority, and is often depicted as a powerful and decisive ruler who is able to command the respect of others.

The fourth Aditya is known as Savitri, who is associated with the concept of knowledge and wisdom. He is revered as the god of learning and enlightenment, and is often depicted as a wise and thoughtful deity who seeks to impart knowledge and understanding to others.

The fifth Aditya is known as Pusan, who is associated with the concept of nourishment and sustenance. He is revered as the god of agriculture and fertility, and is often depicted as a nurturing and supportive deity who helps to provide for the basic needs of the people.

The sixth Aditya is known as Tvashtar, who is associated with the concept of creativity and innovation. He is revered as the god of art and craftsmanship, and is often depicted as a talented and ingenious deity who helps to inspire and guide others in the creative process.

The seventh Aditya is known as Vishvakarman, who is associated with the concept of creation and construction. He is revered as the god of engineering and architecture, and is often depicted as a skilled and resourceful deity who helps to design and build the structures that shape the world.

The eighth Aditya is known as Amshuman, who is associated with the concept of endurance and perseverance. He is revered as the god of strength and courage, and is often depicted as a resilient and determined deity who helps to inspire others to persevere in the face of challenges.

The ninth Aditya is known as Mitra, who is associated with the concept of friendship and alliance. He is revered as the god of diplomacy and cooperation, and is often depicted as a friendly and conciliatory deity who helps to foster relationships and build bridges between different groups.

The tenth Aditya is known as Varuna, who is associated with the concept of justice and righteousness. He is revered as the god of law and order, and is often depicted as a fair and impartial deity who helps to ensure that the laws of the universe are upheld.

The eleventh Aditya is known as Ansa, who is associated with the concept of abundance and prosperity. He is revered as the god of abundance and good fortune, and is often depicted as a generous and benevolent deity who helps to provide for the needs of the people.

The twelfth and final Aditya is known as Vivasvant, who is associated with the concept of light and illumination. He is revered as the god of the sun and the bring light, warmth, and life to the world. He is often depicted as a radiant and shining deity, whose rays of light bring hope and vitality to all those who bask in his glow.

In Hindu mythology, the Adityas are revered as powerful and benevolent deities, who are responsible for maintaining balance and order in the world. They are seen as protectors and guardians, who help to guide and support the people on their journey through life. Whether it is through bringing prosperity and abundance, or through imparting knowledge and wisdom, the Adityas are revered as powerful and benevolent deities who help to enrich and enrich the lives of those who honor and worship them.

CHAPTER FOUR

The Rudras: the eleven deities of destruction

The Rudras are a group of 11 deities in Hinduism who are associated with the vital energies or "pranas" that animate the human body, as well as the human soul. The names of the ten pranas are Praana, Apaana, Vyaana, Samaana, Udaana, Naag, Kurma, Krikal, Devadutta, and Dhananjaya. These pranas are nervauric forces that are believed to be responsible for various functions within the human body, such as breathing, digestion, and circulation. The eleventh Rudra is the human soul, which is believed to be the source of consciousness and the essence of a person's being.

The Rudras are a group of 11 deities in Hinduism who are associated with the vital energies or "pranas" that animate the human body, as well as the human soul. These deities are revered for their role in sustaining and nourishing the human body, and are seen as protectors and guardians of the natural order.

The first Rudra is known as Praana, who is associated with the vital energy of life and breath. He is revered as the god of life and vitality, and is often depicted as a powerful and vital deity who helps to sustain and nourish the human body.

The second Rudra is known as Apaana, who is associated with the vital energy of elimination and excretion. He is revered as the god of purification and cleansing, and is often depicted as a gentle and soothing deity who helps to rid the body of toxins and impurities.

The third Rudra is known as Vyaana, who is associated with the vital energy of circulation and movement. He is revered as the god of circulation and flow, and is often depicted as a powerful and vital deity who helps to sustain and nourish the human body.

The fourth Rudra is known as Samaana, who is associated with the vital energy of digestion and assimilation. He is revered as the god of digestion and nourishment, and is often depicted as a gentle and nurturing deity who helps to provide for the basic needs of the body.

The fifth Rudra is known as Udaana, who is associated with the vital energy of expansion and growth. He is revered as the god of growth and development, and is often depicted as a powerful and vital deity who helps to sustain and nourish the human body.

The sixth Rudra is known as Naag, who is associated with the vital energy of motion and movement. He is revered as the god of motion and agility, and is often depicted as a swift and graceful deity who helps to guide and support the body on its journey through life.

The seventh Rudra is known as Kurma, who is associated with the vital energy of transformation and renewal. He is revered as the god of transformation and renewal, and is often depicted as a powerful and vital deity who helps to sustain and nourish the human body.

The eighth Rudra is known as Krikal, who is associated with the vital energy of perception and awareness. He is revered as the god of perception and awareness, and is often depicted as a wise and insightful deity who helps to guide and support the body on its journey through life.

The ninth Rudra is known as Devadutta, who is associated with the vital energy of communication and expression. He is revered as the god of communication and expression, and is often depicted as a eloquent and persuasive deity who helps to guide and support the body on its journey through life.

The tenth Rudra is known as Dhananjaya, who is associated with the vital energy of victory and success. He is revered as the god of victory and success, and is often depicted as a powerful and victorious deity who helps to guide and support the body on its journey through life.

The eleventh and final Rudra is known as Aja, who is associated with the vital energy of life and regeneration. He is revered as the god of life and regeneration, and is often depicted as a powerful and vital deity who helps to sustain and nourish the human body.

In Hindu mythology, the Rudras are revered as powerful and benevolent deities who are responsible for sustaining and nourishing the human body and soul. They are seen as protectors and guardians, who help to guide and support the people on their journey through life. Whether it is through providing nourishment and sustenance, or through bringing victory and success, the Rudras are revered as powerful and benevolent deities who help to enrich and enrich the lives of those who honor and worship them.

The concept of the 33 Koti Devata consists of eight Vasu, eleven Rudra, twelve Aditya, one Indra, and one Prajapati. The Rudras are the ten Pranas, or nervauric forces, which inhabit the human body. The eleventh Rudra is the human soul, the life force that animates us all.

The 33 Koti Devata concept has been elucidated in the preceding chapters in detail. However, there are still numerous forms of deity concepts in Hinduism that I am endeavoring to explore for a convenient reference.

CHAPTER FIVE

The Trimurti: Brahma, Vishnu, and Shiva

The Trimurti, or the three gods Brahma, Vishnu, and Shiva, play an important role in Hindu mythology. The Trimurti is unique among divine trios, since each of its three members has distinct functions and is revered as a powerful deity, allowing them to transcend simple association and form a unified idea. It is this combination of three distinct personalities and roles that allows for the multifaceted approach to religious and meditative practices that Hindu culture is known for.

Brahma, often depicted as four-headed, is responsible for the creation of the universe and is known for his fierce intelligence and infinite knowledge. Together with Saraswati, the Goddess of knowledge and creativity, he works to maintain order in the world. He is the keeper of the four Vedas, the ancient Hindu scriptures, and is often sacrificed to in order to gain understanding or enlightenment.

The second member of the Trimurti is **Vishnu**, who is often portrayed with four arms, a blue skin, and holding a conch and a discus. His role is to maintain order, protect the righteousness within the world and destroy evil. He is also seen to be responsible for reincarnating himself in a series of avatars in order to further accomplish his purpose. The most famous of his avatars is the divine hero Rama, who slew the wicked demon-king Ravana and whom many Hindus worship as a divine being.

The final member of the Trimurti is **Shiva**, known for his great power, meditation, and ability to destroy. He is often personified as the destroyer, but ultimately is seen as a being of both creation and destruction, representing the building and dissolving of ideas, forms and worlds. He is depicted with a single head, three eyes, and a cobra around his neck, often with a trident in one hand and a drum in the other. Shiva is the great teacher of spiritual knowledge, credited with the authorship of several Hindu scriptures.

The combination of Brahma, Vishnu, and Shiva creates the Trimurti, a perfect synthesis of creativity, preservation, and destruction. Within these individual roles each of these gods takes upon themselves the responsibility of helping maintain harmony within the universe and providing a path to spiritual understanding for Hindus everywhere. The Trimurti thus provides three distinct yet interconnected paths to a higher understanding of life, making it a vital part of Hinduism.

CHAPTER SIX

The Navagrahas: the nine celestial deities

The Navagrahas, also known as the "Nine Celestial Deities," are a group of nine deities in Hinduism who are each associated with a specific planet or celestial body. These deities are believed to have a powerful influence on the lives of human beings and are often invoked in rituals and prayers for their blessings and protection.

Each of the Navagrahas is associated with a specific planet or celestial body, as well as with certain characteristics and qualities. For example, the Navagraha Surya is associated with the sun and is revered as a deity of light, warmth, and energy. The Navagraha Chandra is associated with the moon and is revered as a deity of emotion, sensitivity, and fertility. The Navagraha Mangala is associated with Mars and is revered as a deity of courage, strength, and passion.

In Hindu tradition, the Navagrahas are believed to have a powerful influence on the lives of human beings. They are seen as representing the nine dimensions of human experience, including health, wealth, relationships, and spiritual growth. As such, the Navagrahas are often invoked in rituals and prayers for blessings and protection, and their symbols are often displayed in homes and businesses as a way to bring good fortune and success.

The Navagrahas are an important part of Hinduism and are revered by many Hindus as powerful and benevolent deities. They are seen as symbols of the forces of the cosmos and the natural order, and they are believed to be able to bring prosperity, good fortune, and happiness to those who honor them. Whether through ritual, prayer, or simply by displaying their symbols in one's home or business, the Navagrahas are a powerful and enduring presence in the Hindu tradition.

The Navagrahas, also known as the "Nine Celestial Deities," are a group of nine deities in Hinduism who are each associated with a specific planet or celestial body. The names of the Navagrahas are:

Surya - associated with the sun

Chandra - associated with the moon

Mangala - associated with Mars

Budha - associated with Mercury

Brihaspati - associated with Jupiter

Shukra - associated with Venus

Shani - associated with Saturn

Rahu - associated with the ascending lunar node

Ketu - associated with the descending lunar node

Each of the Navagrahas is associated with certain characteristics and qualities, and they are revered as powerful and benevolent deities in Hinduism. They are often invoked in rituals and prayers for blessings and protection, and their symbols are often displayed in homes and businesses as a way to bring good fortune and success.

CHAPTER SEVEN

The Dikpalas: the eight deities of the cardinal directions

The Dikpalas, also known as the Lords of the Directions, are an archaic phenomenon rooted in Indian mythology. Before the grand pantheon of gods was born, these seven Dikpalas were charged with protecting the world from chaos and calamity. In Hinduism, it is believed that the world is composed of seven directions--east, west, north, south, northeast, southeast, and northwest. To divide the world into these seven directions and protect them from chaos, each direction was given a separate and unique guardian.

The Dikpalas are typically depicted in Indian art as powerful and majestic avatars, representing aspects of the natural world as well as divine and spiritual elements. Each Dikpala is also associated with one of the seven primary chakras, thereby connecting their power to the cosmic energy matrix that lies within us all. According to legends, the Dikpalas were first created by Lord Vishnu and are responsible for maintaining universal balance and order.

The seven Dikpalas are Indra (East), Agni (South-East), Yama (South), Varuna (West), Vayu (North-West), Kubera (North), and Isana (North-East). Indra is known as the leader of the gods and wields thunderbolts and foresight. Agni is associated with fire and knowledge, and is said to be the origin of the sacred fire rituals in Hinduism. Yama is the lord of death and is often depicted as riding a buffalo. Varuna is the lord of water and is responsible for the cosmic ocean and the monsoon. Vayu is the lord of wind and presides over all forms of movement. Kubera is the god of wealth and is believed to be the guardian of all wealth, material and spiritual. Finally, Isana is the god of healing, and anyone seeking release from disease or suffering is believed to call on Isana's power.

The Dikpalas are an ancient concept that still remains relevant in Hindu mythology today. These powerful lords of the directions are thought to bring stability and balance to the world, and their power remains as strong and vital as ever. From protection against evil forces to providing spiritual guidance and connecting us to the cosmic chakras, the Dikpalas serve as important deities in Hinduism.

CHAPTER EIGHT

The Yakshas and Yakshinis: the nature deities

The Yakshas and Yakshinis are a class of nature deities in Hinduism who are associated with natural phenomena such as mountains, forests, and rivers. These deities are often depicted as powerful and protective figures, and they are revered as guardians of the natural world.

The Yakshas are male nature deities, while the Yakshinis are their female counterparts. Both the Yakshas and Yakshinis are often depicted as having human-like bodies with animal heads or features, symbolizing their connection to the natural world. They are also often depicted holding weapons or other symbols of power, indicating their protective nature.

There are many Yakshas and Yakshinis in Hindu mythology, each with their own specific areas of influence and associations. Some of the more well-known Yakshas and Yakshinis include:

Kubera - the Yaksha king and god of wealth, associated with the mountain of Kailash and the precious metal gold.

Vasuki - the Yaksha king of serpents, associated with the river Ganges and the mineral poison.

Manibhadra - the Yaksha king of the Yakshas, associated with the forest and the mineral emerald.

Chanda-Munda - the Yaksha general and chief of the Yakshas, associated with the mountains and the mineral ruby.

Manasa - the Yakshini queen of serpents, associated with the river Padma and the mineral poison.

Dharani - the Yakshini queen of the Yakshinis, associated with the earth and the mineral coral.

The Yakshas and Yakshinis are an important part of Hinduism and are revered as powerful and protective deities. They are seen as symbols of the forces of nature and the natural world, and they are believed to be able to bring prosperity, good fortune, and happiness to those who honor them. Whether through ritual, prayer, or simply by displaying their symbols in one's home or business, the Yakshas and Yakshinis are a powerful and enduring presence in the Hindu tradition.

CHAPTER NINE

The Gandharvas: the celestial musicians

The Gandharvas are a class of celestial deities in Hinduism who are associated with music and the arts. These deities are often depicted as handsome and talented musicians and are revered as patrons of the arts and as bringers of joy and beauty to the world.

According to Hindu mythology, the Gandharvas were a group of celestial beings who were created at the beginning of time to sing and play music in honor of the gods. They were believed to possess great musical talent and were often depicted playing instruments such as the lute and the flute. In addition to their musical skills, the Gandharvas were also said to be incredibly handsome and charming, and they were known for their love of dancing and revelry.

In Hindu tradition, the Gandharvas are revered as deities of music and the arts, and they are often invoked in rituals and prayers for inspiration and creativity. They are also sometimes depicted on the walls of temples and other sacred spaces, serving as guardian deities and sources of beauty and joy.

There are many Gandharvas mentioned in Hindu mythology, each with their own specific associations and characteristics. Some of the more well-known Gandharvas include:

Hamsa - the king of the Gandharvas and a celestial musician, associated with the swan and the element of air.

Chitraratha - the chief of the Gandharvas and a celestial musician, associated with the parrot and the element of fire.

Tumburu - a celestial musician and one of the most famous Gandharvas, associated with the element of earth.

Narada - a celestial musician and sage, known for his ability to travel between the earthly and celestial realms.

Panchajanya - a celestial musician and one of the sons of the god Krishna.

Visvavasu - a celestial musician and the leader of a group of Gandharvas known as the Visvavasus.

The Gandharvas are revered as deities of music and the arts in Hinduism and are often invoked in rituals and prayers for inspiration and creativity. They are also sometimes depicted in Hindu art and mythology as handsome and talented musicians, bringing joy and beauty to the world through their music and art.

The Gandharvas are an important part of Hinduism and

are revered by many Hindus as powerful and benevolent deities. They are seen as symbols of the beauty and power of the arts, and they are believed to be able to bring prosperity, good fortune, and happiness to those who honor them. Whether through ritual, prayer, or simply by enjoying and appreciating the arts, the Gandharvas are a powerful and enduring presence in the Hindu tradition.

CHAPTER TEN

The Vahanas: the sacred animals of the devatas

In Hindu mythology, the Vahanas represent a diverse swath of animals that serve as divine messengers and carriers for the devatas, or gods and goddesses. Vahanas are depicted as being spiritual in nature and are seen as being an extension of service to their divine masters. They serve as a symbol of the divine's capacity for transcendence, which allows them to traverse the physical and spiritual realms of creation.

Vahanas are traditionally presented as animals, but they also often take on human forms, reflecting the wide range of creatures associated with the devatas. Common animal vahanas include the lion, elephant, cow, and eagle, all of which symbolize different aspects of the gods' powers. In some cases, even plants can take on vahana status; for instance, the sacred lotus is associated with the goddess Lakshmi.

The presence of these divine beasts in Hindu mythology

is intricately linked to their religious significance. A few of the most recognizable are related to particular gods, such as the elephant for Ganesha or the lion for Durga. Each of these animals has long been associated with traits and characteristics associated with their assigned god or goddess.

In addition to specific deities, vahanas can be seen as embodiments of the gods and goddess themselves. As agents of divine forces, they are a representation of the transcendent nature of the gods and goddesses. On a more prosaic level, they can be seen as companions to the gods and goddesses, beings that confer strength, protection, and blessing.

Whether animal or human-like, these vahanas are presented as faithful servants that are ever vigilant and devoted to their masters. They have a special place in Hindu mythology, both in terms of their mythology and their spiritual significance. As agents of the gods and goddesses, they are seen as sacred entities that can invoke divine powers. In this way, their presence is intimately tied to the presence of their divine masters in Hindu mythology.

The Apsaras: the celestial dancers

The Apsaras are celestial dancers found widely throughout Hinduism, Buddhism, and Jainism. These female spirits are believed to have descended from the heavens with graceful powers, and hold a special place in the religious, artistic, and cultural realms of ancient India and Southeast Asia.

Apsaras are usually depicted as beautiful female figures, elegantly dressed in silks and bejeweled clothing, with semi-human and semi-divine traits. They are often characterized as having long, flowing hair, fair skin, slanted eyes, and thin waists. In some stories, Apsaras are depicted with wings and are said to have marine-like tails. They are said to have bewitched people who hear their music and stare into their beautiful eyes.

The Apsaras, in their entirety, bear witness to the violent yet captivating power of both divine and temporal beauty. While they are said to possess immortalistic qualities, they are often portrayed as leaving the mortal realm to reside in the heavens above. The Apsaras are linked to the sublimity of nature, carrying on even after the gods perished. Theirs can be an identity apart from the majority culture, allowing the marginalized to be empowered and accepted.

In heavenly painting and temple sculptures, Apsaras are seen to be dancing around the gods, entertaining them and helping to shift their moods. They are also closely connected with sacred texts such as the Rig Veda and the Bhagavad Gita; Apsaras are often mentioned in sacred lyrics and in folklore telling the stories of their celestial beauty.

An interesting point about Apsaras is that, although they are largely viewed as female deities, there are stories that depict male forms of these spirits as well. It is said that these "male" Apsaras were just as beautiful, if not more so than the women, and that their grace was unparalleled in the eyes of the gods.

Apsaras have a distinct presence even to this day. Symbols representing them are often found in jewelry, art, and household decorations. They are embodied in stories, each one possessing its own unique beauty. Music, poetry and dance, all embodying characteristics of the Apsaras, continue to remain at the heart of Indian culture.

From the majestic legend of the Deva and their Apsaras to the age-old Indian mythology, the Apsaras are described as beautiful beyond words, ready to leave their heavenly kingdom to help those in need. The Apsaras put a spell on those that gaze upon their beauty and entice them to become part of the otherworldly realm. In this way, the celestial dancers provide us with an insight into our own eternal beauty.

CHAPTER TWELVE

The Kinnaras and Kimpurushas: the semi-divine beings

The Kinnaras and Kimpurushas are mythical semi-divine beings from Hindu mythology. Both realm from the realm of the gods, playing a significant role in the universe, and have held great spiritual significance for thousands of years.

Kinnaras are half-human and half-equine creatures, having the head of a human and the body of a horse. They have been described as being incredibly beautiful, and are thought to be guardians of the heavens and servants of the gods. According to Hindu scripture, they are associated with music, singing, and dance, playing the veena (a North Indian classical stringed instrument) before Lord Indra, the god of the heavens. Devotion and loyalty to the gods is also attributed to the Kinnaras, with them being described in literature as full of honour and dignity. In terms of physical characteristics, they are said to have a shiny red aura, four hands, and sometimes a third eye in the middle of their forehead.

Kimpurushas are similar to Kinnaras, in that they are semi-divine creatures, but their physical form is different. Instead of appearing as human-horse hybrids, they are human-bird hybrids, with the head and trunk of a human, and the wings and claws of a bird. They are thought to be commonly associated with wisdom and knowledge, and appear in Hindu mythology as wise advisors and teachers. They are said to have excellent prophetic powers, and have been known to protect virtuous people and advise them on their actions. Also, as with the Kinnaras, Kimpurushas are thought to have an incredibly beautiful appearance, and the ability to create music with their wings.

The Kinnaras and the Kimpurushas have both been of great spiritual significance in Hindu mythology for thousands of years. They have both played a prominent role in the universe, with Kinnaras being associated with music and loyalty to the gods, and Kimpurushas being associated with wisdom and knowledge. Both also have excellent physical characteristics, such as reddish auras and strong wings, making them truly semi-divine creatures.

CHAPTER THIRTEEN

The Asuras: the demons and anti-gods

The Asuras are a class of deities in Hinduism who are associated with chaos, destruction, and the forces of darkness. These deities are often depicted as demons or anti-gods, and they are revered as powerful and fearsome figures.

According to Hindu mythology, the Asuras were a group of deities who were born from the sweat of the god Brahma. They were said to be powerful and fierce, and they were often at war with the gods, who represented order and light. Despite their negative reputation, however, the Asuras were also revered as symbols of strength, power, and determination.

There are many Asuras mentioned in Hindu mythology, each with their own specific associations and characteristics. Some of the more well-known Asuras include:

Hiranyakashipu - the king of the Asuras and a powerful demon, known for his attempt to kill the god Vishnu.

Hiranyaksha - the brother of Hiranyakashipu and a powerful demon, known for his attempt to steal the earth and bring it down to the underworld.

Rahu - a demon who is associated with the ascending lunar node and is known for causing eclipses.

Ketu - a demon who is associated with the descending lunar node and is known for causing eclipses.

Virochana - the son of Hiranyakashipu and a powerful demon, known for his attempt to overthrow the gods.

The Asuras are an important part of Hinduism and are revered as powerful and fearsome deities. They are seen as symbols of chaos and destruction, and they are often depicted in Hindu art and mythology as demons or anti-gods. Despite their negative reputation, however, the Asuras are also revered as symbols of strength, power, and determination, and they are often invoked in rituals and prayers for protection and strength. So, they have a dual nature, both positive and negative.

CHAPTER FOURTEEN

The Rakshasas: the malevolent spirits

The Rakshasas have been present in Indian mythology since ancient times. Referred to as powerful and malevolent spirits, these creatures are believed to have descended from Brahma and inhabit faraway lands and exotic realms. Unseen by most humans, the Rakshasas have the power to shape-shift and create illusion, making them one of the most powerful 'ghouls' of Indian folklore.

Rakshasas are said to have a variety of characteristics and abilities. Depending on the story, they may be described as winged and/or horned giants, possessing either immense strength, great intelligence, or both. In some stories, Rakshasas are described as semi-immortal and capable of entering another's dreams and read their minds. Depending on the tale, the Rakshasas may also wield supernatural powers such as flight, invisibility, and teleportation.

Rakshasas are believed to be typically malevolent towards humans, especially when provoked. In their folklore, the Rakshasas are depicted as the antagonists. They are usually depicted as tormenting heroes and heroines, preying upon travelers, building obstacles for the heroes to overcome in their quests, and causing chaos and destruction in villages. Though they are often depicted as being powerful and dangerous, the Rakshasas can also display more benevolent, affectionate, and helpful traits to individuals they deem worthy.

In addition to their dark, malicious nature, the Rakshasas have also been thought to have a spiritual presence. In Hinduism, they are regarded as Eeshvara Bhuta, or forms of God and are believed to have a particular power in the afterlife. It is also said that those who are killed by a Rakshasa will never be able to ascend to heaven.

In many ways, the Rakshasas represent a universal figure of chaos and darkness, one that stands in opposition to human values, ethics, and morality. Though these creatures are often thought of as terrible and evil, they are an important part of Indian mythology. They serve as a reminder of the potential for malevolence, yet also the potential for redemption and hope. In this way, they serve as a useful story-telling device and a reminder of the ever-present struggle between good and evil.

CHAPTER FIFTEEN

The Pishachas: the flesh-eating demons

The Pishachas are malevolent demons who originate from Hindu mythology and are thought to originate from East India. They are known to feed on human flesh, leading them to be considered one of the most terrifying creatures in Indian culture.

The Pishachas are described as ghoulish, often unsettling apparitions, who exist mostly in the spiritual realm. They have a human-like form and pale white skin, with long blue hair and two large eyes that often glow red ominously. It is believed that they are typically invisible to most humans but can be seen by those who have supernatural powers. The Pishachas are also known to lurk around graveyards, forests, and water crossings, where they often feed on the flesh of living animals and humans.

In addition to their physical characteristics, the Pishachas are thought to have identifying magical and alchemical powers that make them even more feared by humans. These include the power of invisibility, shape shifting, and possession. Some believe that these demons can manipulate people's thoughts and feelings, taking control of their life and making them do potentially dangerous things for their own benefit.

The Pishachas are thought to be summoned by performing various rituals, such as offering incense, chanting spells, or making sacrifices. The intention is to call upon the Pishacha's dark powers to remove obstacles, gain knowledge, or to manipulate the outcome of a certain situation. However, spiritual practitioners warn against summoning these demonic forces as they can be incredibly dangerous.

The Pishachas are feared primarily because of their voracious appetite for flesh. They are believed to consume the flesh of not only animals and humans but also corpses. This characteristic has made them the focus of endless horror stories, with some accounts saying that when the Pishachas are summoned, they are unable to be controlled and will attack whoever is nearby.

Though feared by many, the Pishachas are still seen as a powerful force in Indian mythology and believed to bring great knowledge and insight to those who possess the ability to summon them. Whether used for good or evil, the Pishachas are one of the most dangerous and powerful creatures in Indian folklore.

The Bhutas: the ghosts and spirits

The Bhutas are a class of deities in Hinduism who are associated with ghosts, spirits, and the forces of the underworld. These deities are often depicted as fearsome and malevolent figures, and they are revered as powerful and potentially dangerous entities.

According to Hindu mythology, the Bhutas are the spirits of the dead who have not yet been reincarnated. They are said to roam the earth, haunting the living and causing chaos and destruction. Despite their negative reputation, however, the Bhutas are also revered as powerful and potentially helpful deities, and they are often invoked in rituals and prayers for protection and strength.

There are many Bhutas mentioned in Hindu mythology, each with their own specific associations and characteristics. Some of the more well-known Bhutas include:

Bhuta-Ganas - a group of ghostly spirits who are associated with the god Shiva and are known for causing chaos and destruction.

Pretas - the spirits of the dead who are stuck in the earthly realm and are known for causing hauntings and possession.

Vetalas - the spirits of the dead who are said to inhabit corpses and are known for causing hauntings and possession.

Pisachas - the spirits of the dead who are associated with the forest and are known for causing hauntings and possession.

Rakshasas - the spirits of the dead who are associated with the underworld and are known for causing chaos and destruction.

The Bhutas are an important part of Hinduism and are revered as powerful and potentially dangerous deities. They are seen as symbols of the forces of the underworld and the supernatural, and they are often depicted in Hindu art and mythology as ghosts, spirits, and malevolent entities. Despite their negative reputation, however, the Bhutas are also revered as powerful and potentially helpful deities, and they are often invoked in rituals and prayers for protection and strength.

CHAPTER SEVENTEEN

The Pretas: the hungry ghosts

The Pretas are a class of deities in Hinduism who are associated with hungry ghosts, spirits of the dead who are stuck in the earthly realm and are unable to move on to the next life. These deities are often depicted as emaciated and ghostly figures, and they are revered as powerful and potentially dangerous entities.

According to Hindu mythology, the Pretas are the spirits of the dead who were not able to fulfill their desires or obligations in life. They are said to roam the earth, haunting the living and causing chaos and destruction. The Pretas are also said to be constantly hungry and thirsty, and they are often depicted as having huge stomachs and tiny mouths, symbolizing their insatiable hunger and thirst.

There are many Pretas mentioned in Hindu mythology, each with their own specific associations and characteristics. Some of the more well-known Pretas include:

Kui-Yi - a Preta who is associated with the Chinese

underworld and is known for causing hauntings and possession.

Yama-no-Kami - a Preta who is associated with the Japanese underworld and is known for causing hauntings and possession.

Pisacha - a Preta who is associated with the forest and is known for causing hauntings and possession.

Rakshasa - a Preta who is associated with the underworld and is known for causing chaos and destruction.

Vetala - a Preta who is said to inhabit corpses and is known for causing hauntings and possession.

The Pretas are an important part of Hinduism and are revered as powerful and potentially dangerous deities. They are seen as symbols of the forces of the underworld and the supernatural, and they are often depicted in Hindu art and mythology as emaciated and ghostly figures. Despite their negative reputation, however, the Pretas are also revered as powerful and potentially helpful deities, and they are often invoked in rituals and prayers for protection and strength.

CHAPTER EIGHTEEN

The Vetalas: the vampire-like spirits

The Vetalas, or Vetalakas, are a type of mischievous revenant or vampire-like spirit in Hindu mythology. A Vetala is typically a humanoid creature that resides in charnel grounds, haunted places, crossroads, and graveyards. They are known for being mischievous and sometimes dangerous.

The Vetalas are believed to be cursed souls who are stuck in a limbo state between life and death and are unable to move on. They are thought to be created from those who perform cruel acts or who cause death and suffering in their lives, such as those who commit suicide or murder. These cursed souls are then reanimated in the form of a Vetala.

Though traditionally seen as malevolent spirits, Vetalas also have benevolent aspects as well. In some tales, a Vetala is said to have the ability to grant wishes and even help fulfill them. They are said to have wisdom and knowledge beyond what a human can comprehend. In some cases, they are even seen as benefactors, helping people to find lost items, providing them with a wealth of knowledge and wisdom, and helping to bring self-fulfillment.

The Vetalas are sometimes seen as helpful spirits, and in some stories they are even said to help the gods on certain occasions. This could be in the form of providing assistance or advice to adventurers or heroes in need. However, Vetalas can also be dangerous and mischievous. Some stories portray them as predators who attack and consume unsuspecting victims, or as pranksters who would garb themselves in a false identity in order to trick their prey into believing them to be a harmless human.

Despite their often-malicious nature, the Vetalas are still part of the Hindu pantheon, and are generally regarded as both benevolent and malevolent forces. The Vetalas' supernatural strength and powers offer the possibility of great rewards or great danger, depending on how they are treated. As such, Vetalas have become an important part of Indian folklore, and have been present in many stories, legends, and artwork over the centuries.

CHAPTER NINETEEN

The Brahmarakshasas: the powerful demon spirits

The Brahmarakshasas are a class of deities in Hinduism who are associated with powerful demon spirits. These deities are often depicted as malevolent and fearsome figures, and they are revered as powerful and potentially dangerous entities.

According to Hindu mythology, the Brahmarakshasas are the spirits of the dead who were once powerful Brahmins (priests) or scholars. They are said to have been cursed by the gods for misusing their knowledge or power, and as a result, they have been transformed into demon spirits. The Brahmarakshasas are said to be incredibly powerful and are known for causing chaos and destruction.

There are many Brahmarakshasas mentioned in Hindu mythology, each with their own specific associations and characteristics. Some of the more well-known Brahmarakshasas include:

Brahmarakshasa - the leader of the Brahmarakshasas and a powerful demon spirit.

Aghasura - a Brahmarakshasa who took the form of a serpent and was slain by the god Krishna.

Dhenuka - a Brahmarakshasa who took the form of a donkey and was slain by the god Krishna.

Keshi - a Brahmarakshasa who took the form of a horse and was slain by the god Krishna.

Kravyada - a Brahmarakshasa who took the form of a boar and was slain by the god Vishnu.

The Brahmarakshasas are an important part of Hinduism and are revered as powerful and potentially dangerous deities. They are seen as symbols of the forces of the underworld and the supernatural, and they are often depicted in Hindu art and mythology as malevolent and fearsome figures. Despite their negative reputation, however, the Brahmarakshasas are also revered as powerful and potentially helpful deities, and they are often invoked in rituals and prayers for protection and strength.

CHAPTER TWENTY

The Dharmapalas: the guardian deities of dharma

The Dharmapalas are a class of deities in Hinduism who are associated with dharma, the moral and spiritual laws that govern the universe. These deities are often depicted as powerful and protective figures, and they are revered as guardians of dharma and as bringers of justice and righteousness.

According to Hindu mythology, the Dharmapalas are the guardians of dharma, charged with protecting the moral and spiritual laws that govern the universe. They are said to be incredibly powerful and are often depicted as fierce and formidable warriors, ready to defend dharma against any threats. The Dharmapalas are also said to be the enforcers of justice, ensuring that those who violate dharma are punished and those who uphold dharma are rewarded.

There are many Dharmapalas mentioned in Hindu mythology, each with their own specific associations and characteristics. Some of the more well-known Dharmapalas include:

Yama - the god of death and the chief of the Dharmapalas, associated with justice and righteousness.

Virudhaka - a Dharmapala who is associated with the earth and is known for enforcing justice and righteousness.

Virupaksha - a Dharmapala who is associated with the sky and is known for enforcing justice and righteousness.

Dhrtarastra - a Dharmapala who is associated with the wind and is known for enforcing justice and righteousness.

Vaishravana - a Dharmapala who is associated with the mountain and is known for enforcing justice and righteousness.

The Dharmapalas are an important part of Hinduism and are revered as powerful and protective deities. They are seen as symbols of dharma, the moral and spiritual laws that govern the universe, and they are often depicted in Hindu art and mythology as fierce and formidable warriors, ready to defend dharma against any threats. The Dharmapalas are also revered as bringers of justice and righteousness, and they are often invoked in rituals and prayers for protection and guidance.

CHAPTER TWENTY-ONE

The Kalki avatar: the final incarnation of Vishnu

In Hindu religion, the Kalki avatar of Vishnu is worshipped as the last incarnation of the deity. According to Hindu texts, the Kalki avatar will arrive at the end of the Kali Yuga to reestablish righteousness and morality on Earth.

The Kalki avatar is said to possess superhuman power, arrive riding a white horse, have a blazing sword in his hand and be accompanied by a host of divine servants. He is believed to be the warrior king of Surya Vamsa (Solar Dynasty), and will bring about the end of the Kali Yuga. He will be the saviour of humans and will establish a new era of truth and knowledge in the world.

The Kalki avatar is also said to possess four major aims in its mission on Earth, which include destroying evil, freeing the innocent and the destitute, restoring faith and destroying those who are against morality. He will achieve these aims through the destruction of the wicked and his own superhuman powers. Hindus believe that this destruction will bring about the end of the Kali Yuga and the beginning of the Satya Yuga, a golden age of truth and knowledge.

The Kalki avatar will also bring a new set of rules and regulations to govern society and promote unity and harmony. He will introduce a new social order and a new set of governing principles to ensure justice and equality in the world. He is said to be the embodiment of righteousness and true justice, and the protector of the righteous.

It is believed that, after destroying all evil, the Kalki avatar will usher in a new era of harmony and knowledge, in which people will be free from suffering, and can live in true peace and happiness. The Kalki avatar will be the last incarnation of Vishnu, and there are no more iterations of Vishnu after him.

At the end of the Kali Yuga, Vishnu's Kalki avatar will emerge from the heavens and be the ultimate saviour for humanity. He will bring about the end of an era of suffering and will establish eternal truth and justice on Earth. Hindus believe that this will bring about a new era of peace, harmony, and abundance.

Other Books Of The Author

1. The Moments When I Met God
2. Kashiyile Theertha Pathangal
3. GURU GYAN VANI
4. Abhiprerak Gita
5. ASSI SE JAIN GHAT TAK
6. Hopelessness of Arjuna
7. The Soul and It's True Nature
8. Sense of Action (Karma)
9. Action through Wisdom
10. Action through Wisdom
11. THEORY AND PRACTICAL OF EVERY ACTION
12. LOGICAL UNDERSTANDING OF THE SUPREME
13. THE IMPERISHABLE SUPREME
14. Yatra Nishadraj se Hanuman Ghat Tak
15. Yatra Karnatak Ghat se Raja Ghat Tak
16. Yatra Pandey Ghat se Prayagraj Ghat Tak
17. Yatra Ranjendra Prasad Ghat se Dattatreya Ghat Tak
18. YaatraSindhiya Ghat se Gwaliar Ghat Tak
19. Yatra Mangala Gauri Ghat se Hanuman Gadhi Ghat Tak
20. Yatra Gaay Ghat Se Nishad Ghat Tak
21. MAA GANGA, GHATEN EVM UTSAV
22. Ganga Arti Dev Deepavali evam Any Utsav
23. Potentials of Digitalized India
24. VEDIC CONSCIOUSNESS
25. A Brief Introduction to Vedic Science
26. Kashi ke Barah Jyotirling
27. IMPACT OF MOTIVATION
28. Let's have a Milky Way Journey
29. Color Therapy in a Nutshell

30. Rigveda in a Nutshell
31. Yajurveda in a Nutshell
32. Samveda in a Nutshell
33. Atharva Veda in a Nutshell
34. Ayushman Bhava - Ayurveda
35. Srimad Bhagavad Gita and Upanishad Connection
36. Srimad Bhagavad Gita - an attempt to summarize each chapter.
37. Facts and Impact of Nakshatra
38. Astro Gems - NAVARATNA
39. Ekadashi - A Concise Overview
40. A Concise View of Hanuman Chalisa
41. Inspirational Gita
42. Nakshatraranyam
43. Summary of 18 Mahapuranas
44. Synopsis of 18 Upa Puranas
45. Rigvediya Upanishads
46. Shukla Yajurvediya Upanishads
47. Krishna Yajurvediya Upanishads
48. Samavediya Upanishads
49. Atharvavediya Upanishads
50. The Seven Great Sages
51. From Rocket Scientist to President Dr. APJ Abdul Kalam
52. The Visionary's Voice - Quotes of Dr. APJ Abdul Kalam
53. The Wisdom of Swami Vivekananda: Insights and Inspiration from a Legendary Spiritual Teacher
54. Ayurvedic Remedies from the Garden
55. Sages and Seers
56. Rising Strong – Motivational Stories of Women
57. Beyond Flames -Mystery stories of Funeral Ghat Manikarnika
58. The Origins of Tulsi: A Look at the Mythological Roots of the Plant"

59. "The Holistic Cow: A Look at the Physical, Spiritual, and
     Cultural Importance of Cows in India"
60. The Art of Healing "Art Therapy"

• 57 •

Contact

DR. JAGADEESH PILLAI

PhD in Vedic Science

Four Times Guinness World Record Holder

Winner of Mahatma Gandhi Vishwa Shanti Puraskar and
Global Peace Ambassador

Gemology, Astro & Vastu Consultant - Spiritual Counselor

Consultant for designing World Record Ideas

Efficient Tarot Card Reader

9839093003

myrichindia@gmail.com

drjagadeeshpillai@facebook

drjagadeeshpillai@instagram

jagadeeshpillai@youtube

www. JAGADEESHPILLAI.com

|| LOKAHA SAMASTHAHA SUKHINO BHAVANTU ||

• 61 •